What's in this book

This book belongs to

_____

音乐家莫扎特
The musician Mozart

学习内容 Contents

背景介绍：
第2至3页分别是四个伟大音乐家的雕塑。

沟通 Communication

说出乐器名称
Say the names of some
musical instruments

说说音乐家莫扎特
Talk about the great
musician Mozart

莫扎特（Wolfgang Amadeus Mozart,
1756–1791），欧洲最伟大的古典主义音乐
作曲家之一。

生词 New words

★ 音乐	music
★ 拉	to play
★ 小提琴	violin
★ 聪明	clever
★ 容易	easy
★ 难	difficult
★ 礼物	present
★ 小时候	when I was small
★ 小时	hour
★ 正在	while, in the process of
钢琴	piano
弹	to play
歌剧	opera

巴赫（Johann Sebastian
Bach, 1685–1750），被称作
"音乐之父"，经典作品有《马
太受难曲》、《约翰受难曲》等。

瓦格纳（Richard Wagner, 1813–1883），
创作了《尼伯龙根的指环》和《特里斯坦与
伊索尔德》等经典乐剧。

句式 Sentence patterns

姐姐正在弹钢琴。
My sister is playing the piano.

文化 Cultures

认识中国乐器
Learn about Chinese musical instruments

贝多芬（Ludwig van Beethoven,
1770–1827），经典曲目有《第五交
响曲"命运"》和《月光奏鸣曲》等
等，被称为"乐圣"。

跨学科学习 Project

认识声音是如何产生的，制作水杯木琴
Learn how sound is produced and make a water
glass xylophone

参考答案：
1 Yes, I do./No, I like pop music.
2 I know the person in the last picture is Beethoven./
No, I do not know any of them.
3 Yes, I love his music./I might have.

Get ready

1 Do you like classical music?

2 Do you know the people in the pictures?

3 Have you heard any music composed by Mozart?

yīn yuè
音乐

cōng ming
聪明

xiǎo shí hou
小时候

"聪明"用来形容一个人智力高，理解和记忆事物的能力强。

参考问题和答案：
1 Do you know this boy? (Yes, he is Mozart, a great musician./No.)
2 Was Mozart good at music when he was small? (Yes, he was good at music that people called him a music prodigy.)
3 Do you think Mozart is clever? (Yes, I think so.)

故事大意：
本课介绍了音乐家莫扎特杰出的音乐才华及其短暂的一生。

你知道莫扎特吗？他很聪明，在他小时候，人们都叫他音乐神童。

参考问题和答案

1 Who is this girl? What is she doing? (This girl is Mozart's elder sister. She is playing the piano.)

2 What is Mozart doing? (Mozart is watching his sister and learning how to play the piano.)

3 Has Mozart learnt how to play the piano? (Yes, he has learnt to play simple melody.)

róng yì
容易

gāng qín
钢琴

tán
弹

zhèng zài
正在

"正在"表示某一动作在进行中。

有一天，姐姐正在弹钢琴，他在旁边看，学会了容易的曲子。

莫扎特很努力，每天弹几个小时钢琴，很快就会弹很难的曲子。

参考问题和答案：

1 What is Mozart doing? (He is learning to play the violin from his father.)
2 What is Mozart writing? (He is composing his first opera.)

他还跟爸爸学习拉小提琴。十几岁的时候，他就写了第一部歌剧。

莫扎特写了很多优秀的作品，他在各地的表演也都很成功。

参考问题和答案：
Do people from different places love Mozart's works and performances? (Yes, they do.)

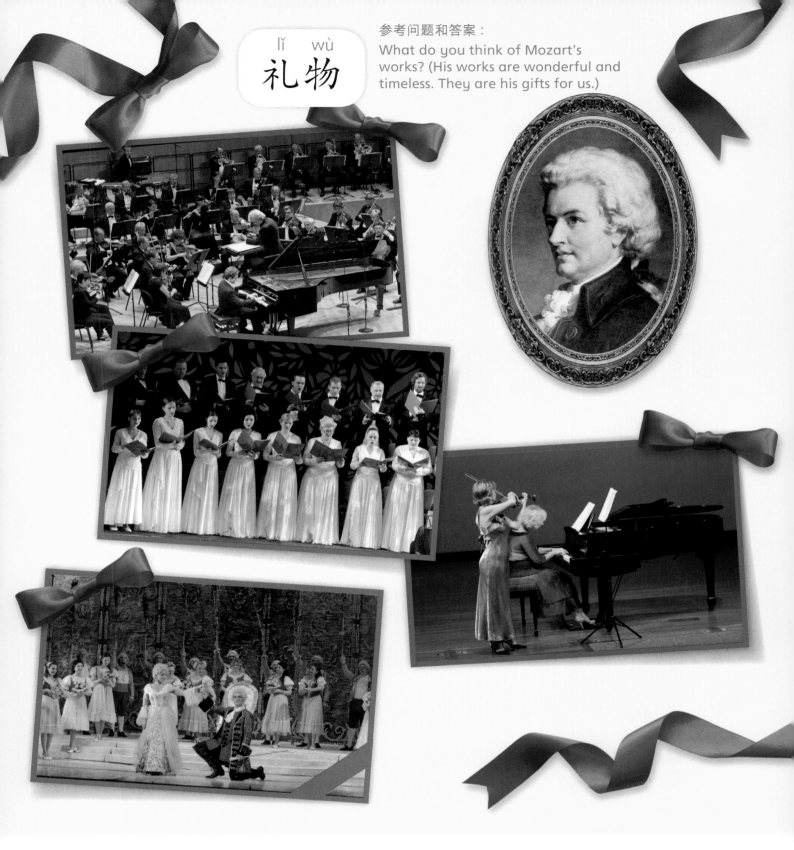

参考问题和答案：
What do you think of Mozart's works? (His works are wonderful and timeless. They are his gifts for us.)

莫扎特35岁就去世了。这些作品都是他留给我们的礼物。

莫扎特 1756 年出生，英年早逝于 1791 年。他擅长创作协奏曲、奏鸣曲、交响曲和歌剧等，后成为古典音乐的代表。其作品经典不朽，至今仍然充满活力。

Let's think

1 Recall the story. Number the pictures in order. 提醒学生回忆故事，观察第4至9页。

3

1

2

4

2 Do you like music? Discuss what music you like and don't like with your friend. 参考表达见下方。

我喜欢音乐，因为我觉得钢琴曲很好听。

你喜欢音乐吗？为什么？

我喜欢……
因为……

我不喜欢……
因为……

我喜欢音乐，因为我喜欢我的音乐老师。

我不喜欢拉小提琴，因为太难了！

New words

1 Learn the new words.

延伸活动：
复习生词，并让学生用这些词试着复述莫扎特的故事，或者说
说自己学音乐的经历。如"莫扎特小时候很聪明。有一天，他
姐姐正在弹钢琴……""我六岁开始学习拉小提琴……"

提醒学生注意固
定搭配："弹钢
琴""拉小提琴"。

2 Listen to your teacher and point to the correct words above.

"小时"是时间单
位，"小时候"指年
纪小的一段时间。

11

1 Listen and circle the correct letters.

 2 Look at the pictures. Listen to the story an...

1 星期六，浩浩做了什么？
  a 去爷爷家玩
  b 去办公室上班
  (c) 弹钢琴

2 玲玲去年的生日礼物是什么？
  (a) 小提琴
  b 蛋糕
  c 钢琴

3 伊森和艾文要做什么？
  a 听音乐
  b 看电影
  (c) 看歌剧

 星期五学校音乐节，你们唱歌还是跳舞？

 你等着看伊森、艾文和我的歌剧吧！

你们呢？

我弹钢琴，姐姐唱歌，还有布朗尼跳舞。

 歌剧会不会很难唱？

 不太难。伊森和艾文正在音乐室唱歌，我现在也要去那里。

 布朗尼会跳舞？它真聪明！

它现在正在跟姐姐一起跳舞呢！

学生完成练习后，老师总结"正在"的用法：
"人/事＋正在＋动作"。

3 Complete the sentences and role-play with your friend.

> a 给她打针
> b 看报纸　c 刷牙

医生正在做什么？

小女孩生病了，医生正在 __a__ 。

爷爷和奶奶正在做什么？

爷爷和奶奶正在一起 __b__ 。

已经七点了，快来吃早饭，上学要迟到了。

我正在 __c__ ，快好了。

Task

让学生上网或看书搜集自己喜欢的音乐家的资料，并带照片回来，向同学介绍。鼓励学生在听了同学的分享后，可向其发问，通过交流提高中文表达能力。

Who is your favourite musician? Do some research and talk about him/her with your friend.

我很喜欢……

Paste your photo here.

他叫莫扎特，他很聪明，十几岁就会写歌剧。今天，还有很多人非常喜欢他的音乐。你听过他写的歌剧吗？我很喜欢。你可以上网去听听。

Game

Play with your friends. Count the number of piano keys below in Chinese. Who can do it faster?

黑色的有多少个？
白色的有多少个？

一、二、三……

……十四、十五、十六……

黑色的有……个，白色的有……

黑色的有 **18** 个，白色的有 **26** 个。

Chant

🎧 05 **Listen and say.** 说唱到"拉提琴"和"弹钢琴"的时候，学生做相应的动作。

莫扎特小神童，
聪明认真无人比，
能拉提琴弹钢琴，
能写歌剧和乐曲。
莫扎特音乐家，
努力优秀又年轻，
世界各地去表演，
留下很多好作品。

生活用语 Daily expressions

真聪明！
So clever!

太难了。
It's so difficult.

写一写 Write

1 Trace and write the characters.

丶 亠 亠 立 产 咅 咅 音

一 匚 乐 牙 乐

音	乐	音	乐
音	乐		

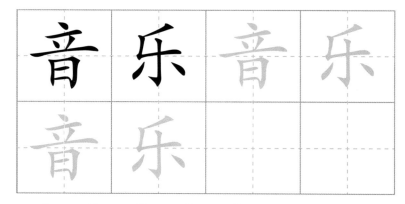

一 丁 下 正 正

一 ナ ナ 在 在 在

告诉学生中国人在计数时，常使用"正"字，一个"正"字代表"五"，两个"正"字代表"十"，依此类推，方便易懂。

正	在	正	在
正	在		

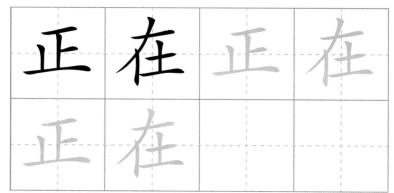

2 Write and say.

我很喜欢听<u>音乐</u>，我每天会听一个小时。

他们是五年级的学生，<u>正在</u>教室里考试。

16

3 Read and circle the correct words.
先让学生整体阅读，理解段落内容，再选择正确的词，最后通读完成后的段落。

今天放学后，我和姐姐一起去（音乐室/图书馆）学习拉（提琴/钢琴）。

我和姐姐拉的提琴不一样，我拉大提琴，姐姐拉小提琴。我学习大提琴快半年了，我觉得它很（难/容易）拉，我应该好好学习。姐姐四岁的时候开始学习小提琴，她很（聪明/漂亮），老师新教的音乐，她拉了一个多（小时/小时候）就会了。你想听我和姐姐一起（弹/拉）提琴吗？

拼音输入法 Pinyin input

Write the letters in the correct blanks to complete the passage.
Then type the whole passage.

| a 中间还写着 莫扎特的姓名 | b 更喜欢莫扎特 的音乐 | c 还在这里弹 琴、写歌剧 |

八月的时候，爸爸带我去参观了莫扎特住过的房子。

这所房子是黄色的，有很多窗户，__a__。爸爸说，莫扎特住在这里，__c__。

我很喜欢这所房子，但是我__b__。

答题技巧：
第一空所在句子讲的是房子的外观，故选 a。第二空是讲莫扎特住在这里的生活。最后一空是总结性的，且 b 中的"更喜欢"与前半句的"喜欢"相对应。

多元学习 Connections

Cultures

老师介绍完中国古典乐器之后，可播放一些古典乐器演奏的乐曲，让学生感受中国古典音乐的魅力，以及与西方音乐的不同。

1 The traditional Chinese musical instruments usually fall into four types. Learn about them.

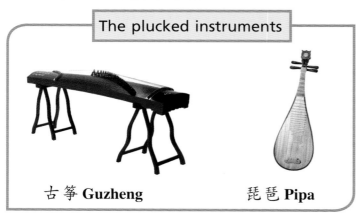

The plucked instruments

古筝 Guzheng

琵琶 Pipa

The majority of the traditional Chinese instruments are made of wood, bamboo and leather.

Chinese instruments are either played solo, in small ensembles or in large orchestra .

The bowed instruments

二胡 Erhu

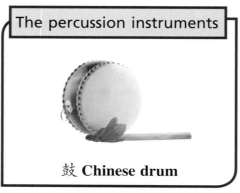

The percussion instruments

鼓 Chinese drum

The wind instruments

笛子 Dizi

除了讨论图片中的内容，学生还可以说说自己听过哪些乐器演奏的中国古典音乐。也可说说自己在学校学习了什么乐器。

2 Chinese children usually learn to play traditional music at school. Talk about these pictures with your friend.

她正在弹《赛马》(Horse Racing）这个音乐吗？

我不知道，但是中国音乐很好听，我喜欢。

除了书中的实验，老师还可以让学生触摸自己声带的位置，感受说话发出声音时的震动。最后老师总结：声音是通过物体（气态、固态、液态）震动产生的。

1 Do you know how sound is produced? Do an experiment and learn about it.

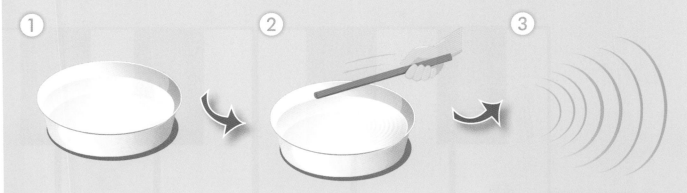

① **Fill a bowl with water.**
一个装有水的脸盆（脸盆材质较薄时，实验效果更佳）。

② **Strike the bowl, watch the water vibrate.**
用一根筷子或者棍子敲打脸盆的边缘。

③ **Sound is produced by vibration.**
在敲打脸盆发出声音的同时，可以发现水面因震动产生了波纹。

2 Make a water glass xylophone. Perform to your friend.

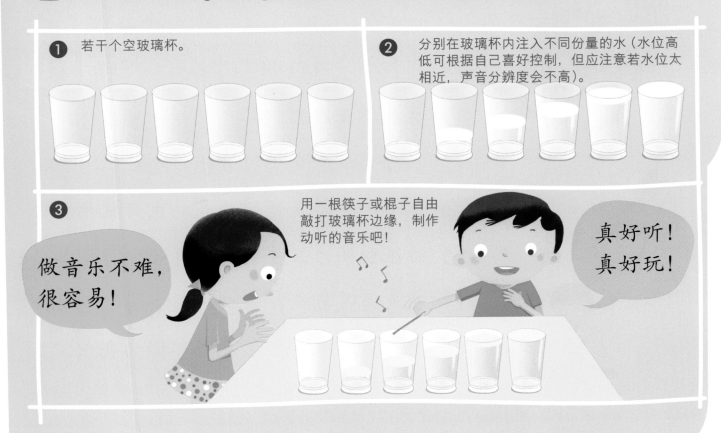

① 若干个空玻璃杯。

② 分别在玻璃杯内注入不同份量的水（水位高低可根据自己喜好控制，但应注意若水位太相近，声音分辨度会不高）。

③ 用一根筷子或棍子自由敲打玻璃杯边缘，制作动听的音乐吧！

做音乐不难，很容易！

真好听！真好玩！

温习 Checkpoint

学生每回答一题，就可弹奏标有相应题号的琴键，最后可得出按题号顺序所演奏的是 do do so so la la so，是《一闪一闪亮晶晶》(Twinkle, Twinkle, Little Star) 或《字母歌》(Alphabet Song) 中的一段旋律。

1 Write the characters and say the sentences aloud. Then play the piano keys as numbered. Can you guess which music note you played?

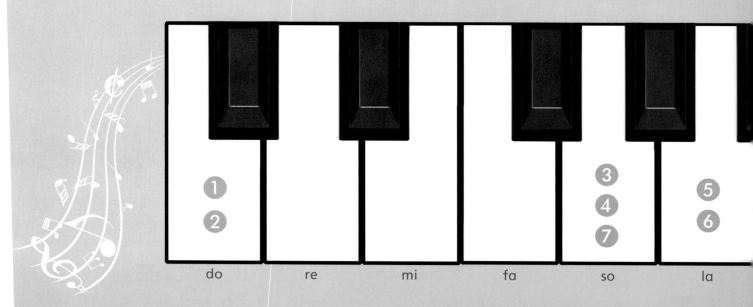

do   re   mi   fa   so   la

① 你会不会写 music 的中文字？　音　乐

② 莫扎特正在弹钢琴。

③ 我每天听一个小时音乐。

④ 这个小提琴是妈妈给我的生日礼物。

⑤ 她很聪明，三岁的时候开始学弹钢琴。

⑥ 明天是星期六，我们一起去看歌剧吧！

⑦ 长大了我也想做莫扎特那样的音乐家。

学生两人一组，互相考察评价表内单词和句子的听说读写。交际沟通部分由老师朗读要求，学生再互相对话。如果达到了某项技能要求，则用色笔将星星或小辣椒涂色。

2 Work with your friend. Colour the stars and the chillies.

Words and sentences			
音乐	☆	☆	☆
拉	☆	☆	🌶
小提琴	☆	☆	🌶
聪明	☆	☆	🌶
容易	☆	☆	🌶
难	☆	☆	🌶
礼物	☆	☆	🌶
小时候	☆	☆	🌶
小时	☆	☆	🌶
正在	☆	☆	☆
钢琴	☆	🌶	🌶
弹	☆	🌶	🌶
歌剧	☆	🌶	🌶
姐姐正在弹钢琴。	☆	☆	🌶

Say the names of some musical instruments	☆
Talk about the great musician Mozart	☆

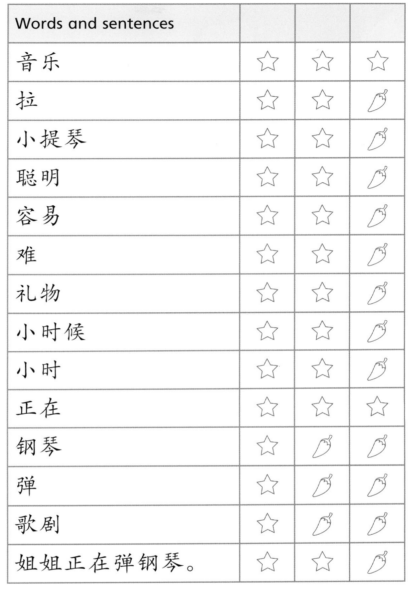

si

3 What does your teacher say?

评核建议：
根据学生课堂表现，分别给予"太棒了！
(Excellent!)"、"不错！(Good!)"或"继续
努力！(Work harder!)"的评价，再让学生圈
出右侧对应的表情，以记录自己的学习情况。

21

分享 Sharing

Words I remember

音乐	yīn yuè	music
拉	lā	to play
小提琴	xiǎo tí qín	violin
聪明	cōng ming	clever
容易	róng yì	easy
难	nán	difficult
礼物	lǐ wù	present
小时候	xiǎo shí hou	when I was small
小时	xiǎo shí	hour
正在	zhèng zài	while, in the process of
钢琴	gāng qín	piano
弹	tán	to play
歌剧	gē jù	opera

Other words

神童	shén tóng	prodigy
曲子	qǔ zi	melody

延伸活动：
1 学生用手遮盖英文，读中文单词，并思考单词意思；
2 学生用手遮盖中文单词，看着英文说出对应的中文单词；
3 学生四人一组，尽量运用中文单词分角色复述故事。

努力	nǔ lì	to make efforts
就	jiù	already
跟	gēn	with
部	bù	volume
优秀	yōu xiù	outstanding
作品	zuò pǐn	composition
各地	gè dì	everywhere
表演	biǎo yǎn	performance
成功	chéng gōng	successful
去世	qù shì	to pass away
留	liú	to leave
乐器	yuè qì	musical instruments
古筝	gǔ zhēng	guzheng
琵琶	pí pa	pipa
二胡	èr hú	erhu
鼓	gǔ	Chinese drum
笛子	dí zi	dizi

OXFORD
UNIVERSITY PRESS

Oxford University Press is a department of the University of Oxford.
It furthers the University's objective of excellence in research, scholarship,
and education by publishing worldwide. Oxford is a registered trade mark of
Oxford University Press in the UK and in certain other countries

Published in Hong Kong by
Oxford University Press (China) Limited
39th Floor, One Kowloon, 1 Wang Yuen Street, Kowloon Bay,
Hong Kong

© Oxford University Press (China) Limited 2017

Illustrated by Ah Lun, Anne Lee, Emily Chan, KY Chan and Wildman

Photographs for reproduction permitted by Dreamstime.com

China National Publications Import & Export (Group) Corporation is an authorized distributor of
Oxford Elementary Chinese.

Please contact content@cnpiec.com.cn or 86-10-65856782

ISBN: 978-0-19-082311-5

10 9 8 7 6 5 4 3 2

Teacher's Edition
ISBN: 978-0-19-082323-8

10 9 8 7 6 5 4 3 2